Gran

I am giving you this book as I would love to hear all about you, your lifetime and all the special memories that you have created over the years.

I hope you will enjoy reading through the questions, writing the answers, and reminiscing about your wonderful life journey. I would love to hear all about your memories, from your childhood and formative years through to your current thoughts and feelings.

Please know that when you have finished answering the questions and return this book to me, I will treasure it and its contents forever. I love you always.

To: Nan

From: Claire

xxx

What is your full name? Do you know why this name was chosen for you?

Where were you born, and what is your date of birth?

Were your parents strict? Were you good or did you used to get in trouble all the time?

Do you look more like your Mum or your Dad? Are there traits that run in the family, such as height or dark hair?

_____

_____

_____

_____

_____

_____

_____

_____

_____

_____

_____

_____

_____

_____

_____

_____

Did you know your aunts, uncles and grandparents when you were growing up? What are your memories of them?

_____

_____

_____

_____

_____

_____

_____

_____

_____

_____

_____

_____

_____

_____

_____

_____

What is your first memory?

_____

_____

_____

_____

_____

_____

_____

_____

_____

_____

_____

_____

_____

_____

_____

_____

_____

_____

If you have brothers and sisters, please tell me their names and the year in which they were born.

What is your favourite memory of your Mum, and of your Dad? Did you get on better with one of them than the other?

_____

_____

_____

_____

_____

_____

_____

_____

_____

_____

_____

_____

_____

_____

_____

_____

Tell me about your first house: where was it, and for how long did you live there? How many rooms did it have, and did you like it?

Was religion important to you and your family? If so, please tell me all about it: did you have a strict religious upbringing? Is religion still important to you now?

_____

_____

_____

_____

_____

_____

_____

_____

_____

_____

_____

_____

_____

_____

_____

Are there any family heirlooms? If so, what are they?

_____

_____

_____

_____

_____

_____

_____

_____

_____

_____

_____

_____

_____

_____

_____

_____

_____

_____

What is your fondest memory of childhood?

Are there any funny or memorable stories that were handed down the family? If so, I'd love to hear about them please.

Tell me about Christmas when you were growing up: was it a big family event? Did you have any traditions? A favourite Christmas carol?

_____

_____

_____

_____

_____

_____

_____

_____

_____

_____

_____

_____

_____

_____

_____

_____

_____

Did you have a favourite toy when you were young? Why did you like it? What were the most popular toys and fashions of the era?

_____

_____

_____

_____

_____

_____

_____

_____

_____

_____

_____

_____

_____

_____

_____

_____

_____

Tell me about your school: what was it called, and where was it?

How many other places have you lived in during your life? Tell me all about them

_____

_____

_____

_____

_____

_____

_____

_____

_____

_____

_____

_____

_____

_____

_____

_____

_____

They say that your schooldays are the happiest days of our lives. Is that your experience or did you not really like school? I'd love to know all about your school days.

What was your favourite school subject, and what was your least favourite subject?

What did you want to be when you grew up?

Did you have to wear a school uniform? If you did, can you please describe it?

What personality did you have as a child: were you loud and always out having fun, or did you prefer activities like reading on your own?

_____

_____

_____

_____

_____

_____

_____

_____

_____

_____

_____

_____

_____

_____

Did you have many friends growing up? What was the name of your best friend? Are you still in contact with your oldest friends?

Do you remember if you used to get pocket money? If so, what did you like to spend it on? Did you try to save it or always spend it?

_____

_____

_____

_____

_____

_____

_____

_____

_____

_____

_____

_____

_____

_____

_____

What sort of things did you do outside of school when you were younger? Who were the most popular bands, and who were the famous celebrities and sporting icons at the time?

_____

_____

_____

_____

_____

_____

_____

_____

_____

_____

_____

_____

_____

_____

Did you have any posters on your wall as a child? If so, who were they, and why did you like them?

_____

_____

_____

_____

_____

_____

_____

_____

_____

_____

_____

_____

_____

_____

_____

_____

Do you speak any other languages, if so which ones and how well do you speak them?

At what age did you leave school, and did you go to university afterwards? If so, which one did you go to and did you enjoy it? I'd love to know all about what you did after leaving school.

_____

_____

_____

_____

_____

_____

_____

_____

_____

_____

_____

_____

_____

Did you have any hobbies? What were they, and why did they appeal to you?

_____

_____

_____

_____

_____

_____

_____

_____

_____

_____

_____

_____

_____

_____

_____

_____

_____

_____

Did you like going to discos when you were younger? Are you a good dancer, and what is your favourite dance?

_____

_____

_____

_____

_____

_____

_____

_____

_____

_____

_____

_____

_____

_____

Do you like sport? If so, what was your favourite sport when you were growing up and why? Did you play any sports for fun or even competitively?

_____

_____

_____

_____

_____

_____

_____

_____

_____

_____

_____

_____

_____

_____

Do you have a party trick? If yes, what is it?

_____

_____

_____

_____

_____

_____

_____

_____

_____

_____

_____

_____

_____

_____

_____

_____

Were you ever on TV or in a newspaper? If so, what for.

_____
_____
_____
_____
_____
_____
_____
_____
_____
_____
_____
_____
_____
_____
_____
_____
_____
_____

Do you have a favourite memory or day that you can tell me about?

_____

_____

_____

_____

_____

_____

_____

_____

_____

_____

_____

_____

_____

_____

_____

_____

_____

Would you say you are an emotional person, or do you prefer to keep things to yourself?

_____

_____

_____

_____

_____

_____

_____

_____

_____

_____

_____

_____

_____

_____

_____

_____

_____

Are you an organised person? Do you like to plan in advance, or do you prefer to be spontaneous?

_____

_____

_____

_____

_____

_____

_____

_____

_____

_____

_____

_____

_____

_____

_____

_____

_____

Did you have a honeymoon? If so where did you go and for how long? Was it memorable?

_____

_____

_____

_____

_____

_____

_____

_____

_____

_____

_____

_____

_____

_____

_____

_____

_____

_____

If you were or are married, tell me all about your spouse: when and how did you meet; was it love at first sight? What are your memories of your wedding day and life together?

Tell me all about the time you became a parent. Were you nervous before the birth? Did you know what to expect? Was looking after a child what you expected it to be?

_____

_____

_____

_____

_____

_____

_____

_____

_____

_____

_____

_____

_____

_____

_____

Do you have a proudest moment or memory, as a parent?

What are your memories of me as a child?

_____

_____

_____

_____

_____

_____

_____

_____

_____

_____

_____

_____

_____

_____

_____

_____

_____

_____

How many children did you have in total? What are their names and ages? I'd love to hear all about your family life.

_____

_____

_____

_____

_____

_____

_____

_____

_____

_____

_____

_____

_____

_____

_____

_____

Have I changed over the years?

_____

_____

_____

_____

_____

_____

_____

_____

_____

_____

_____

_____

_____

_____

_____

_____

_____

_____

Do you prefer to spend money, or to save it? Did managing money come easily to you?

_____

_____

_____

_____

_____

_____

_____

_____

_____

_____

_____

_____

_____

_____

_____

How many different jobs have you had, and which was your favourite and which one did you like the least? Did you enjoy your working life?

Do you like to read books? What is your favourite type of book to read and why? Who is your favourite author?

Do you enjoy watching films? Do you have a favourite film, and a favourite actor or actress? Who are they, and why?

_____

_____

_____

_____

_____

_____

_____

_____

_____

_____

_____

_____

_____

_____

_____

_____

_____

_____

_____

Do you like music? What type of music do you like the best, and who were your favourite band?

_____

_____

_____

_____

_____

_____

_____

_____

_____

_____

_____

_____

_____

_____

_____

_____

_____

Did you ever play a musical instrument? If so, which one did you play and did you enjoy playing it, and were you good?

_____

_____

_____

_____

_____

_____

_____

_____

_____

_____

_____

_____

_____

_____

_____

_____

Please tell me some of your other favourite things:

Food _____

Drink _____

Game _____

Artist _____

Poet and poem _____

_____

Season _____

What is your most treasured possession, and why?

_____

_____

_____

_____

_____

_____

_____

_____

_____

_____

_____

_____

_____

_____

_____

_____

Do you like to travel? Which countries have you been to, and which is your favourite holiday of all time?

Which major news event do you remember the most vividly during your lifetime? Tell me all about it.

Did you ever have a moment in your life that you considered life-changing? If so, what was it and how did it affect you?

_____

_____

_____

_____

_____

_____

_____

_____

_____

_____

_____

_____

_____

_____

_____

_____

How would you describe yourself?

_____

_____

_____

_____

_____

_____

_____

_____

_____

_____

_____

_____

_____

_____

_____

_____

_____

_____

Looking back, would you say you have had a happy life?

_____

_____

_____

_____

_____

_____

_____

_____

_____

_____

_____

_____

_____

_____

_____

_____

_____

There is a phrase that life is what happens whilst you're busy making other plans. Did your life turn out how you thought it would?

_____

_____

_____

_____

_____

_____

_____

_____

_____

_____

_____

_____

_____

_____

_____

_____

Do you have any regrets or things that you wish you had done differently in your life? If so, what are they?

_____

_____

_____

_____

_____

_____

_____

_____

_____

_____

_____

_____

_____

_____

_____

_____

How would you like others to describe you, and how would you like to be remembered?

What achievements in your life are you most proud of?

Do you think the world is very different now to how it was when you were young? What do you think has changed for the better and what has changed for the worse?

What are you most optimistic about for the future? And what are you most worried about?

_____

_____

_____

_____

_____

_____

_____

_____

_____

_____

_____

_____

_____

_____

_____

_____

_____

Do you think we will ever be visited by aliens? Or are we alone in the universe?

Do you think humanity has a bright future? Will we live on the moon or Mars, and start to explore the galaxy more and more?

Thanks so much for sharing your life story with me, Gran. Have you enjoyed doing so, and do you have any advice for how I live my own life?

_____
_____
_____
_____
_____
_____
_____
_____
_____
_____
_____
_____
_____

Printed in Great Britain
by Amazon

55630934R00047